FIS
BIE

Becoming Women of Purpose

BY RUTH HALEY BARTON

SHAW

WATERBROOK
PRESS

To my parents, Charles and JoAnn Haley, who spoke to me so often about the special package God was putting together in my life that I began to believe them!

Becoming Women of Purpose
A SHAW BOOK
PUBLISHED BY WATERBROOK PRESS
2375 Telstar Drive, Suite 160
Colorado Springs, Colorado 80920
A division of Random House, Inc.

All Scripture quotations, unless otherwise indicated, are taken from the *Holy Bible, New International Version*®. NIV®. Copyright © 1973, 1978, 1984 by International Bible Society. Used by permission of Zondervan Publishing House. All rights reserved. Scriptures marked (NASB) are taken from the *New American Standard Bible*® (NASB). © Copyright The Lockman Foundation 1960, 1962, 1963, 1968, 1971, 1972, 1973, 1975, 1977. Used by permission. (www.Lockman.org) Scriptures marked (PHILLIPS) are taken from The New Testament in Modern English, Revised Edition, © 1972 by J. B. Phillips. Reprinted with permission of the Macmillan Publishing Co., Inc.

ISBN 0-87788-061-1

Copyright © 1992, 1993, revised edition © 2001 by R. Ruth Barton

Printed in the United States of America
2001

10 9 8 7 6 5 4 3 2 1

Contents

elcome to the Women of the Word studyguides—a series especially designed to encourage women in their spiritual journey. No matter what season of life we may be in or how long we have followed Christ, we all face similar issues as women in today's world. Discovering who we are, living in relationship with others, choosing a vocational path, satisfying our spiritual hunger—we women face an unprecedented array of options. At times we are exhilarated by the opportunities, running enthusiastically from option to option like shoppers in a brand-new superstore. At other times we are confused and desperate for guidance—almost paralyzed by a panoply of choices far beyond what women in previous generations could have imagined. We need wisdom that speaks to the complexity of our lives.

Perhaps even deeper than our need for "answers" to life's questions is the desire for an intimate encounter with God. We long for a fresh expression of God's loving concern for us, a sense of personal attention in the midst of an alarmingly impersonal world. And so we approach the Scriptures with high hopes. We know that the Bible is a book like no other— God-breathed not only at the time of its initial writing but also alive and active in the present moment (Hebrews 4:12). Yet we're not always sure how to access it for ourselves. We might wonder, "Will I really have a life-giving encounter with God through the words on these pages, or is that a privilege reserved for others? How do *I* receive the life-changing power that is present in this ancient text?"

One concrete and effective way to open ourselves up to God's work in our lives is through inductive Bible study. This approach involves a dynamic interplay between the mind and the heart. First we engage our minds to read and unravel the meaning of the text. Through careful study and thought, we consider the historical context, explore the meaning of words, concepts, and principles, and reflect on what these might have meant to the original listeners. But the task of observing and interpreting information about the text is just the beginning. It is the "front porch" that leads into the "main house" of our relationship with God. No matter how nice a front porch is, we don't want to stay there forever. We want to be invited to come inside, to get comfortable, to share food and fellowship with the Master of the house. Inductive Bible study offers us just such an invitation—to engage not only our minds but also our hearts as we listen for God's Word for us today.

Our spiritual companions on this journey include the ancient women of the Bible, whose lives bear striking similarities to our own: single women making choices about relationships and lifestyle; young mothers trying to figure out how to balance love for children with other life callings; married women wrestling with the joys and the challenges of long-term commitment; women learning how to answer God's call to service and leadership in the church, the marketplace, and the global community. Regardless of differences in historical and cultural settings, their experiences and life lessons, their successes and failures speak powerfully to our own. Like us, they harbored deep and perhaps inexpressible desires for a life-transforming connection with God. Their lives demonstrate that the God who cared for a slave girl and her baby in the wilderness, answered an infertile woman's prayer, granted wisdom, political savvy, and protection to a Hebrew beauty queen, and extended loving, human touch to women who had looked for love in all the wrong places is the same God who reaches for relationship with us today.

All Scripture, including the stories of those women who have gone before, is given for our instruction, inspiration, and spiritual formation (2 Timothy 3:16). The Women of the Word studyguide series offers you a powerful tool for engaging the Scriptures for spiritual transformation. As you embark on this study, I encourage you to engage your *mind* by being disciplined in your study of historical context, biblical language, and concepts through the notes provided and other trustworthy study materials that you might have on hand. I also encourage you to engage your *imagination* as you reflect on what the biblical teachings might have meant to the women who first heard them. But don't stop there! Take the most courageous step of all by engaging your *heart* and making it your top priority to listen for *God's word to you* in the present moment.

Each time you open God's Word begin with a quiet prayer: "Speak, Lord, for your servant is listening." Trust that he will speak and then, when he does, listen and respond with increasing faithfulness so that you become a woman whose life and character are shaped by the Word.

How to Use This Studyguide

Fisherman studyguides are based on the inductive approach to Bible study. Inductive study is discovery study; we discover what the Bible says as we ask questions about its content and search for answers. This is quite different from the process in which a teacher *tells* a group *about* the Bible—what it means and what to do about it. In inductive study God speaks directly to each of us through his Word.

A group functions best when a leader keeps the discussion on target, but the leader is neither the teacher nor the "answer person." A leader's responsibility is to *ask*—not *tell*. The answers come from the text itself as group members examine, discuss, and think together about the passage.

There are four kinds of questions in each study. The first is an *approach question.* Asked and answered before the Bible passage is read, this question breaks the ice and helps you start thinking about the topic of the Bible study. It begins to reveal where thoughts and feelings need to be transformed by Scripture.

Some of the early questions in each study are *observation questions*—who, what, where, when, and how—designed to help you learn some basic facts about the passage of Scripture.

Once you know what the Bible says, you then need to ask, *What does it mean?* These *interpretation questions* help you to discover the writer's basic message.

Next come *application questions,* which ask, *What does it mean to me?* They challenge you to live out the Scripture's life-transforming message.

Fisherman studyguides provide spaces between questions for jotting down responses as well as any related questions you would like to raise in the group. Each group member should have a copy of the studyguide and may take a turn in leading the group.

A group should use any accurate, modern translation of the Bible such as the *New International Version,* the *New American Standard Bible,* the *New Revised Standard Version,* the *New Jerusalem Bible,* or the *Good News Bible.* (Other translations or paraphrases of the Bible may be referred to when additional help is needed.) Bible commentaries should not be brought to a Bible study because they tend to dampen discussion and keep people from thinking for themselves.

Suggestions for Group Leaders

1. Thoroughly read and study the Bible passage before the meeting. Get a firm grasp on its themes and begin applying its teachings for yourself. Pray that the Holy Spirit will "guide you into all truth" (John 16:13) so that your leadership will guide others.

2. If any of the studyguide's questions seem ambiguous or unnatural to you, rephrase them, feeling free to add others that seem necessary to bring out the meaning of a verse.

3. Begin (and end) the study promptly. Start by asking someone to pray for every participant to both understand the passage and be open to its transforming power. Remember, the Holy Spirit is the teacher, not you!

4. Ask for volunteers to read the passages aloud.

5. As you ask the studyguide's questions in sequence, encourage everyone to participate in the discussion. If some are silent, try gently suggesting, "Let's have an answer from someone who hasn't spoken up yet."

6. If a question comes up that you can't answer, don't be afraid to admit that you're baffled. Assign the topic as a research project for someone to report on next week, or say, "I'll do some studying and let you know what I find out."

7. Keep the discussion moving, but be sure it stays focused. Though a certain number of tangents are inevitable, you'll want to quickly bring the discussion back to the topic at hand. Also, learn to pace the discussion so that you finish the lesson in the time allotted.

8. Don't be afraid of silences; some questions take time to answer and some people need time to gather courage to speak. If silence persists, rephrase your question, but resist the temptation to answer it yourself.

9. If someone comes up with an answer that is clearly illogical or unbiblical, ask her for further clarification: "What verse suggests that to you?"

10. Discourage overuse of cross-references. Learn all you can from the passage at hand, while selectively incorporating a few important references suggested in the studyguide.

11. Some questions are marked with a ◥. This indicates that further information is available in the Leader's Notes at the back of the guide.

12. For further information on getting a new Bible study group started and keeping it functioning effectively, read Gladys Hunt's *You Can Start a Bible Study Group* and *Pilgrims in Progress: Growing Through Groups* by Jim and Carol Plueddemann (both available from Shaw Books).

Suggestions for Group Members

1. Learn and apply the following ground rules for effective Bible study. (If new members join the group later, review these guidelines with the whole group.)

2. Remember that your goal is to learn all that you can *from the Bible passage being studied.* Let it speak for itself without using Bible commentaries or other Bible passages. There is more than enough in each assigned passage to keep your group productively occupied for one session. Sticking to the passage saves the group from insecurity ("I don't have the right reference books—or the time to read anything else.") and confusion ("Where did that come from? I thought we were studying _____.").

3. Avoid the temptation to bring up those fascinating tangents that don't really grow out of the passage you are discussing. If the topic is of common interest, you can bring it up later in informal conversation after the study. Meanwhile, help one another stick to the subject.

4. Encourage one another to participate. People remember best what they discover and verbalize for

themselves. Some people are naturally shy, while others may be afraid of making a mistake. If your discussion is free and friendly and you show real interest in what group members think and feel, the quieter ones will be more likely to speak up. Remember, the more people involved in a discussion, the richer it will be.

5. Guard yourself from answering too many questions or talking too much. Give others a chance to share their ideas. If you are one who participates easily, discipline yourself by counting to ten before you open your mouth!

6. Make personal, honest applications and commit yourself to letting God's Word change you.

Becoming Women of Purpose

An article in a leading newspaper stated that "as Americans we have reached a time when choice, rather than freeing the individual, has become so complex, difficult, and costly that it has become overchoice." And who has been most affected? The modern woman, of course! The article goes on:

> More than half of all women with children are now in the work force, and for them there is an endless barrage of choices over balancing childraising responsibilities, marriage, household duties and career. Social scientists know that with an increase in choices people become more anxious. In fact, it produces guilt, self-doubt, and stress ("The Bane of Democracy," *Chicago Tribune Magazine*, March 10, 1991).

Maybe you see yourself in this description. Perhaps you're wondering, *How can I sift through all my options and make wise choices? How can I avoid coming to the end of my life and regretting the way I chose to spend my time and energy?*

However, other women, rather than feeling that they have

choices, feel very stuck. Even though women do have many options today, our lives are still often filled with the mundane, the ridiculous, the difficult, and the downright tragic. Sometimes it is hard to feel that life has purpose when you spend most of your days scraping modeling clay off the floor, cleaning the bathroom, or working for a boss who doesn't recognize your potential. And the challenges become even more difficult when life itself doesn't seem to have any purpose.

Whether we are overwhelmed by our options or feel limited by our roles, we need to become women of purpose. As we begin to see the unique package God is putting together in our lives and discover his purposes for us as individuals, we will find the framework we need to make wise choices. In addition, we will find that a sense of purpose offers hope in the midst of tragedy and difficulty, gives meaning to the mundane aspects of our lives, and helps us make our lives count for God.

We will begin by exploring God's purposes in creating us, in saving us, and in gifting us. We'll also discover three important elements of purposeful living—identifying God's purposes in our lives, planning for his purposes (goal-setting), and applying this process to specific areas of life at work and home. We end with the assurance that God does not leave us alone but gives us everything we need to accomplish his purposes.

The principles of purposeful living can transform our lives and give us the moorings we need to negotiate the complex and exciting choices we face as women today.

Created for a Purpose

GENESIS 1:24-31; 2:4-7,18-25; PSALM 139:13-16

*Why on earth am I worried about how
I can be somebody? I am somebody,
a unique creation of God.*

—SARAH GUDSCHINSKY

*T*he place to begin in becoming a woman of purpose is at
the beginning—the beginning of the human race and
our own beginnings as individuals. Our purpose is inherent in
our creation. God had a purpose in creating us as human
beings, as women, and as unique individuals. That purpose is
just waiting to be discovered!

1. Name one thing about yourself that makes you
   unique. (You can be as serious or as silly as you
   wish.)

READ GENESIS 1:24-31.

Genesis 1 is an overview of the creation story, while Genesis 2 is a more detailed account of the creation of man and woman.

2. According to these verses, what were God's purposes in creating human beings?

❧3. Why do you think God created us in his image (verse 26), and what does this tell you about the purpose for which we were created?

4. How did God feel about the creation of the human race (verse 31)?

---

5. Reread Genesis 1:26-31, substituting your own name or the personal pronouns *I* or *me* for any of the nouns referring to the human beings God had created (i.e. *man, woman, them, all that he had made*). What does this exercise tell you about God's purpose in creating you as a human being?

READ GENESIS 2:4-7,18-25.

6. In what ways did Eve's creation differ from Adam's?

How was it similar?

7. For what distinct purpose was Eve created?

How did God's method of creating her highlight that purpose?

♈8. Why do you think God created people male and female?

What function in the larger scheme of life is indicated by the physical characteristics of women?

9. In addition to physical characteristics, what are some other differences and similarities you have observed between men and women?

What unique qualities do you, as a woman, bring to your world: your family, your workplace, your neighborhood, and your church?

READ PSALM 139:13-16.

10. What do these verses tell you about God's role in designing you as a unique individual?

How does an understanding of God's role in your formation affect your feelings about yourself and your distinctive characteristics?

Putting It All Together

11. Describe in detail some of the characteristics that make you a unique individual. Include physical characteristics such as appearance and heredity along with temperament, giftedness, likes and dislikes, etc. When do you feel most alive, most fulfilled?

Are you able to accept and enjoy being the person God created you to be? Explain any difficulties you may have with this.

12. What helps you sense that God has a specific and unique purpose for your life? Spend some time brainstorming together about how God could use women like you.

Thank God for creating you just as you are and ask him to show you how he wants to use you—your humanity, your femininity, and your individuality—for his special purposes.

Saved for a Purpose

GENESIS 3; EPHESIANS 1:3-14; 2:4-10

The chief end of [wo]man is to glorify
God and enjoy Him forever.
—THE WESTMINSTER CONFESSION OF FAITH

One of God's purposes in creating Adam and Eve and the entire human race was so that he could have a relationship with us—men and women who were created like him in many ways. However, early in their relationship Adam and Eve disobeyed God, nearly destroying the possibility of fulfilling the greatest purpose of their lives.

In this study we will take a look at the pivotal event in human history that threatened to destroy the most important relationship for which we were created. But we will also see that God had both a plan for restoring that relationship and a purpose for drawing each one of us back to himself. The most important step in becoming women of purpose is to enter into right relationship with the One who created us.

1. Have you ever experienced estrangement in a relationship that was important to you? Were you able to be reconciled with that person? If so, how did that happen?

READ GENESIS 3.

2. What did Satan (speaking through the serpent) say to begin to drive a wedge between God and the human beings he had created?

3. Compare what God actually said (2:16-17) with what Satan reported that he said. Note any inaccuracies.

4. Since Eve clearly understood God's instruction regarding the trees in the garden (3:2-3), what choice did she face? What choice did she make?

5. What were the results of Adam and Eve's choice? Focus particularly on the consequences that affected their relationship with God.

6. Why did God expel Adam and Eve from the Garden (verse 22)?

7. Even in the midst of these sad and disappointing events, what indication is there of God's care and his plan for restoring the human race to a right relationship with himself (verses 15,21)?

Read Ephesians 1:3-14 and 2:4-10 (preferably in more than one translation).

8. God's plan for our salvation, which was only hinted at in Genesis, is fully explained in these New Testament verses. Describe God's plan as you understand it from these verses. Make a note of all the words and phrases that indicate God's purposes in saving us.

9. What seem to be God's overriding motives in his plan of salvation?

How does understanding God's motives affect the way you feel about his plans and purposes?

Putting It All Together

◥10. Have you taken your first step in becoming a woman of purpose by getting into a right relationship with God? If not, see the Leader's Note on pages 66-67 for an explanation of how you can begin this relationship right now.

11. If you are already in a restored relationship with God, you may need to evaluate your life to see if you are presently living according to the purposes presented in these passages. The following questions can help you with this evaluation:

a. Are you taking time to get to know God better, to express your love for him, and to enjoy his presence in your life?

b. How are you growing in your ability to "be holy and blameless before him" so that your life brings praise to him?

c. What aspects of your salvation experience show others "the surpassing riches of his grace"? Are you willing to share your story with others for this very purpose?

d. What are some of the good works that God has prepared for you to do? Are you doing them?

Gifted for a Purpose

1 CORINTHIANS 12:4-31; EPHESIANS 4:11-16

Take that gift God has entrusted to you, and
use it in the service of Christ. He will make it
glow and shine like the very stars of heaven.
—JOHN SUTHERLAND BONNELL

Another important facet of the unique package God is putting together in our lives is the spiritual gifts he gives us through the Holy Spirit. The Bible says that "to each one" God has given a spiritual gift (1 Corinthians 12:7), which is needed in order for the body of Christ to be healthy and whole.

Identifying and using our gifts with an attitude of willing service can give us a wonderful sense of being useful to God and to those around us. We can also be encouraged by knowing that God calls each of us to fulfill a unique role and he will give us the gifts we need to accomplish his purposes for us.

1. How easy or difficult is it for you to believe that you are uniquely gifted? One way to gauge this is how you respond to genuine compliments. Are you able to receive compliments, or do you deflect them?

Read 1 Corinthians 12:4-11 and
Ephesians 4:11-16.

2. Define "spiritual gift."

By whom and to whom are spiritual gifts given?

3. What is the purpose of spiritual gifts (1 Corinthians 12:4-7 and Ephesians 4:11-13)?

    How do you feel about being involved in such a great purpose?

4. As we use our gifts, who is responsible for the results (1 Corinthians 12:6)?

5. List the spiritual gifts mentioned in these passages, then look up these terms in a dictionary or Bible dictionary and write down their definitions.

READ 1 CORINTHIANS 12:12-30.

6. Have you ever looked at other Christians and thought, *They have so much more to offer to the body of Christ than I do?* Have you ever found yourself wishing you had someone else's gifts and abilities? What does Paul's image of the human body and the importance of each part tell you about your value to the body of Christ? (See also Ephesians 4:16.)

7. Who is responsible for "job placement" (verse 18)?

What happens when any one of us fails to contribute according to our giftedness?

Putting It All Together

8. What needs or ministry opportunities are you aware of in your church or community?

Which of these opportunities will you say yes to with a view toward understanding God's purpose for your unique giftedness?

9. Whether you are preparing to serve for the first time or reviewing your past and present ministry experiences, you can learn a lot about what your gifts are by thinking through the following questions:

a. What types of people or needs do I feel most concerned about?

b. What types of ministry do I enjoy and feel ener-
    gized by?

c. In what ministries have I been involved and
    sensed that God was working to bring about
    good results?

d. What natural abilities do I have that could be
    used in a spiritual capacity?

e.   What would I most like to do if it were
      possible?

10.   Summarize the insight you have gained as you have
      reflected on specific ministry experiences or oppor-
      tunities. In what ways is it becoming more apparent
      to you that God has given you specific gifts?

How do you think God might want to use your
gifts in the time and place to which he has brought
you?

Prepared for a Purpose

JOHN 9:1-3; 2 CORINTHIANS 1:3-7; 12:7-10;
HEBREWS 5:7-10

*The experiences of our lives, when we let God
use them, become the mysterious and perfect
preparation for the work He will give us to do.*
—CORRIE TEN BOOM

*A*t this point you may be thinking, *But I'm so limited!
How could God possibly use someone like me for his
great purposes?* Any number of factors can make us feel limited
or inadequate: lack of education or Christian upbringing, a
physical handicap, our marital status (singleness, divorce,
marriage to an unsaved spouse), financial limitations, young
children in the home, or even the way we view our bodies or
our personalities.

However, these are only perceived limitations, not actual
barriers to fulfilling God's purposes. So often, what we see as
limitations are God's training ground for unique ministry

and a showcase for his strength and glory. All of the experiences of our lives—the wonderful ones, the painful ones, and the ordinary ones—are part of God's preparation for the work he has for us.

1. Describe a difficulty or a limitation in your life that ultimately had some good purpose (i.e., it put you in the right place at the right time; resulted in personal growth; prepared you for a future opportunity; etc.).

READ JOHN 9:1-3.

2. What did the disciples assume about the cause of this man's blindness?

What did Jesus say was the purpose of this
"tragedy"?

3. When have you seen "the work of God displayed"
in someone's life as they experienced a tragedy or
difficulty? How did observing God's hand in that
circumstance affect your own life?

READ 2 CORINTHIANS 1:3-7.

4. What aspects of God's character did Paul experience
in a deeper way through his sufferings?

5. What did Paul have to offer to the Corinthians as a result of his suffering?

How do you think his own suffering enhanced his ability to minister to them?

6. When have you endured a difficult situation that caused you to experience God in a new or deeper way? How might God use this experience to help others?

READ 2 CORINTHIANS 12:7-10.

7. If given the opportunity, what one thing about
    yourself or your life would you like to change?

8. Paul had a "thorn in the flesh"—something he
    wanted very much to have removed from his life.
    What was his prayer regarding this thorn?

9. What was God's answer to Paul's prayer?

What was the purpose for this thorn both in Paul's character development (verse 7) and in his ministry (verses 9-10)?

READ HEBREWS 5:7-10.

10. What was Christ's attitude as he prayed to God about the suffering that he was to endure?

What did Jesus learn through his suffering?

❧11. How did his suffering prepare him for his role as our Savior?

Putting It All Together

12. Through this study, what better understanding have you gained of the truth that "in all things God works for the good of those who love him, who have been called according to his purpose" (Romans 8:28)?

How can this understanding change your view of the difficulties you have experienced in the past or may be experiencing now?

13. Although this study has focused primarily on how God uses difficulties to prepare us for ministry, he uses other, more pleasant aspects of life as well: education, God-given opportunities, key relationships, life experience. Jot down some of the ways you believe God has been preparing you and brainstorm about how they ultimately will help you to fulfill his purposes.

If you are experiencing a difficult time right now, don't hesitate to tell God how you feel. Paul and Jesus certainly did! But also ask God to help you see the trial as a tool—one that he can use for good in your life and the lives of others. Thank him for all of the ways, some pleasant and some not so pleasant, by which he is preparing you for his good purpose.

Identifying God's Purposes

ACTS 9:1-19; 26:12-18; PHILIPPIANS 3:12-14

Begin with the end in mind.
—STEPHEN COVEY

*M*any women today are unclear about their ultimate purpose, so they allow people and circumstances to pull them this way and that. Or they have a general idea about what is important to them, but their goals are so poorly defined that it is impossible to tell if they are making any progress.

Becoming the kind of women God wants us to be and accomplishing what he wants us to do will not happen by accident. We need to know what we are aiming for (our purposes), formulate a plan for accomplishing those purposes (our goals), and then discipline ourselves to follow that plan. Paul's life illustrates how each of these three important elements of purposeful living can help us live with confidence that our lives count for God.

1. If you could live any part of your life over again, what would it be? What would you do differently?

READ ACTS 9:1-19 AND 26:12-18.

2. As we have seen in the previous studies, God has a purpose for each of us—a mission, a reason for our existence. What was Paul's mission or purpose?

    Was Paul's understanding of his purpose general or specific?

3. How did Paul come to this understanding of his purpose?

What were some of the key components God used to communicate his purpose to Paul?

READ PHILIPPIANS 3:12-14.

4. Jot down the words and phrases that describe the passion and energy with which Paul focused on living for God's purposes.

5. Paul came to understand his purpose in a very unusual and dramatic way. Few of us will ever receive such an unmistakable revelation, and yet his story encourages us to live with the same sense of purpose he had. What are some of the ways God works today to reveal his purposes for us?

Putting It All Together

6. As you begin to identify God's purposes in your life, you may find it helpful to develop an overall life-purpose statement, a sentence or a paragraph that states the overarching purpose for your life as you have come to understand it. That may sound simple enough, but writing a life-purpose statement can take weeks or months. Once you work through the development process, you'll have a tool that can help you focus your time and energy on what matters most. (See the Leader's Note for some Bible passages to reflect on as you think about your life-purpose statement.)

Developing a life-purpose statement involves:

Prayer—Be open to what God is telling you about yourself.

Thought—Bring together and process the knowledge you already have about your gifts, your opportunities, and your desires.

Time—There is no hurry. God will reveal what you need to know in due time.

Writing—Some people process ideas better through writing; it is also good to record impressions, pertinent Scriptures, and pieces of the puzzle that you gather along the way.

7. After you have developed an overall life-purpose statement, you can prioritize those areas of life through which you will live out your purpose. For most of us this list would include spiritual life, family, church life, vocation, personal development (education, etc.), health, and recreation. Once you clarify which aspects of life have priority, you'll be able to develop a mission statement for each of these areas as well. (See the Leader's Note for a list of scriptures that will help you develop mission statements for these priority areas.)

Note: You'll find a Life-Purpose Statement Worksheet in the back of the book where you can jot down your goals and plans.

Priorities and Planning

PROVERBS 31:10-31; EPHESIANS 5:15-17

Vision without planning is daydreaming.
—ANONYMOUS

We have learned that each of us is created, gifted, and prepared for a specific purpose. It is possible to understand our purpose but still be spending most of our time and energy on other, less important things. Oftentimes we lack a well-defined plan.

As we've seen, a life-purpose statement is by nature very general. So it is also important to identify the specific priority areas through which you will accomplish this mission. In this study we will identify these specific areas and discuss goal setting as a way to incorporate our priorities and purposes into the minutes and hours of our lives. In later studies we will have the opportunity to write down purpose statements in these key areas and develop specific plans for achieving those purposes.

1. Think back to a time when you were confronted
    with a very important task. What did you do to
    make sure you got it done and that you did it right?

READ PROVERBS 31:10-31.

2. How do you feel after reading about the woman
    described here?

3. What words describe this woman?

What was the most important thing about her?

4. What were her areas of responsibility?

5. How do the activities and responsibilities of the Proverbs 31 woman compare with your own?

List your major responsibilities in order of importance to you.

Read Ephesians 5:15-17.

6. The Phillips translation of this passage is helpful:

   Live life, then, with a due sense of responsibility, not
   as [wo]men who do not know the meaning and purpose of life but as those who do. Make the best use
   of your time, despite all the difficulties of these days.
   Don't be vague, but firmly grasp what you know to
   be the will of the Lord.

   What evidence do you find that the Proverbs 31
   woman made the best use of her time?

7. What do you think should be the relationship
   between our sense of purpose and our use of time?

Putting It All Together

A purpose *is an aim or direction, something we want to achieve but which is not necessarily measurable. A* goal, *on the other hand, is a short-term objective that is both accomplishable and measurable and will take us one step closer to our overall purpose.*

8. What are several measurable, accomplishable ways (goals) you can make the best use of your time to accomplish your life purpose?

What does Ephesians 5:17 have to say regarding the process of pursuing our purposes?

9. What signs do you see around you that the days are
   evil (Ephesians 5:16)?

Look again at your goals. How can you reword
them to acknowledge difficulties of your world
without being totally paralyzed by your
situation?

10. What changes can you make that would help give your best time and energy to your highest priorities and purposes?

Exercising Discipline for a Purpose

HEBREWS 12:1-13; 2 TIMOTHY 2:3-7

*Why do we say no? In order to say yes
to what really matters.*

—MIRIAM ADENEY

Setting goals is one thing, but being able to accomplish those goals is quite another! That's where discipline comes in—the discipline to say yes to your plan for accomplishing God's purposes and no to everything that interferes.

1. Can you think of a time when, even though it was hard, you disciplined yourself to accomplish something important? Did the end result make it worthwhile? Share some details.

Read Hebrews 12:1-13.

2. Discipline often involves saying no to things that keep us from accomplishing God's purposes. What kinds of things can slow us down as we run the race and keep us from accomplishing our goals (verse 1)?

3. What positive discipline is mentioned here (verse 2)?

4. How does God's discipline in our lives differ from our own self-discipline?

How does it contribute to our growth as Christians?

5. The writer of Hebrews took care to give an encouraging word to those who are struggling with discipline. He named a common temptation in verse 3. What is it, and how is it visible in the lives of Christians you know or have known?

How does this temptation manifest itself in your life?

6. Consider the discipline you received as a child and explain how it impacted your life.

In what ways is God's discipline of us similar to what you experienced as a child? How is it different?

7. As you look back on your own life, can you identify times when God was disciplining or training you? What lessons did you learn that have helped or could help you accomplish God's purposes?

8. What message to the body of Christ do you find in verses 12-13?

READ 2 TIMOTHY 2:3-7.

9. Here Paul has given three analogies that reveal the importance of self-discipline in the life of a Christian. Although his examples are drawn from his own time and culture, what relevant principles do they offer for us today?

Describe a contemporary illustration of discipline that might be helpful for women today.

Putting It All Together

❧10.　What are some of the hindrances and sins that are slowing you down in your efforts to accomplish God's purposes?

What are some things you need to say no to in order to do what really matters? Identify these by name and ask God for the courage to give them up.

11. What are some of the activities and disciplines that you need to say yes to in order to accomplish God's purposes?

God's Power for His Purposes

2 CORINTHIANS 3:4-6; EXODUS 3–4

God has not given us a spirit of timidity,
but of power and love and discipline.

—2 TIMOTHY 1:7 (NASB)

*I*n writing to the Corinthians about his ministry, Paul asks the question, "And who is adequate for these things?" (2 Corinthians 2:16, NASB). After coming to a deeper understanding of God's purposes for your life, perhaps you are asking the same question. You may be wondering if you have what it takes to live as a woman of purpose.

In this study we will see that when God calls us to accomplish his purposes, he also promises his presence and provides his power every step of the way.

1. How do you feel right now about your ability to live out the purposes, plans, and disciplines you have identified throughout this study?

Read 2 Corinthians 3:4-6.

2. What is Paul's answer to his own question from
   2 Corinthians 2:16, "Who is equal to such a task?"

3. Where should our confidence come from as we live
   out God's purposes?

Read Exodus 3–4.

The life of Moses illustrates the truth that, no matter how inadequate we feel, God will give us all that we need to live according to his purposes.

4. What was the purpose to which God had called
   Moses (3:10)?

❦5. How did Moses respond to this calling? From the
following verses, trace Moses' objections and God's
reassurance.

Moses' Objection	God's Response
Exodus 3:11	3:12
Exodus 3:13	3:14-15
Exodus 4:1	4:2-9
Exodus 4:10	4:11-12
Exodus 4:13	4:14-1

6. Why do you think God became angry with Moses (4:14)?

7. Which of the feelings of inadequacy that Moses expressed can you relate to most easily?

8. How do you think God feels when we allow our feelings of inadequacy to paralyze us and keep us from accomplishing his will?

9. Which of the promises that God gave to Moses are most reassuring to you as you answer his call to live your life for his purposes?

Putting It All Together

10. Read Ephesians 3:20 and Philippians 1:6. Aren't you glad that God does not require us to accomplish his purposes in our own strength? Spend time in prayer admitting to God your feelings of inadequacy. Then examine the Scriptures for promises that reveal your fears are ungrounded. Ask God to give you the spirit of power, love, and self-discipline in place of the spirit of fear (2 Timothy 1:7) so that you can say a resounding "Yes!" to the purposes he has for you.

To end your prayer time, perhaps your group would like to read the following prayer together:

> *Lord, thank you for the unique package you have so carefully put together in my life. I give it back to you today and every day to use as you intended from the moment you created me. I will not be afraid. I will not make excuses. I will say yes to the purposes you've designed specifically for me.*

Leader's Notes

STUDY 1: CREATED FOR A PURPOSE

Question 3. The word *man* as used in Genesis 1:26 is a collective noun referring to humankind as a whole, male and female.

Question 8. There is increasing scientific evidence that not only are men's and women's bodies different, but their brains are different too! Medical studies have shown that between the eighteenth and twenty-sixth week of pregnancy a chemical bath of testosterone and other sex-related hormones wash over a baby boy's brain. This causes the right hemisphere of the brain to recede slightly, destroying some of the connecting fibers. One of the results is that most boys start life with an orientation toward the left side of the brain, which houses more of the logical, analytical, factual, and aggressive centers of thought. On the other hand, girls are less handicapped in their use of the right side of the brain, which is creative, intuitive, and nurturing (Gary Smalley and John Trent, *The Language of Love,* Colorado Springs, Colo.: Focus on the Family Publishing, pp. 35-36).

In light of this discovery, it is interesting to contemplate what unique strengths women can bring to the family, the church, and the workplace.

Question 9. While there are several key differences between men and women that influence life experiences and life purpose, we need to be careful not to overemphasize these differences, a mistake that can lead to stereotypes and obscure the reality of our shared humanity. As Elaine Storkey points out, "We often hear the comment that women and men are the opposite sex. Yet we are more like each other than anything else in creation" (*The Search for Intimacy,* London: Hodder and Stoughton, 1995, p. 119).

For further reading:

Barton, Ruth. *Becoming a Woman of Strength.* Wheaton, Ill.: Shaw Publishers, 1999.

Barton, Ruth. *Equal to the Task: Men and Women in Partnership at Work, at Church, at Home,* chapters 5,6,8, 10. Downers Grove, Ill.: InterVarsity Press, 1998.

Cook, Kaye and Lance Lee, *Men and Women Alone and Together.* Wheaton, Ill.: Victor Books, 1992.

STUDY 2: SAVED FOR A PURPOSE

Question 6. Charles Ryrie notes that "driving Adam and Eve from the garden was both a punishment and an act of mercy lest they should eat of the tree of life and live forever in a state of death and alienation" (Charles Ryrie, ed., Ryrie Study Bible, Chicago: Moody Press, 1976, p. 12).

Question 7. Genesis 3:15 is commonly understood as a prophecy that a descendant of the woman (Christ) would suffer because of Satan (be bruised on the heel by him) but would achieve the ultimate victory by dealing a deathblow to Satan's head at the cross. (See 1 John 3:8.)

Question 10. To begin a personal relationship with Jesus Christ, you need to:

- Confess (agree with God) that you are a sinner (Romans 3:23).
- Realize that God offers forgiveness of sin (1 John 1:9) and the free gift of eternal life (Romans 6:23). He is able to offer this because of the death of his Son, Jesus Christ (John 3:16).
- "Believe in the Lord Jesus, and you will be saved" (Acts 16:31).

If you have never done so, accept God's forgiveness and his gift of eternal life through the death of Jesus Christ by expressing your faith to God in prayer. Be assured that nothing can take away your salvation or separate you from God's love (Romans 8:38-39).

STUDY 3: GIFTED FOR A PURPOSE

Question 2. A spiritual gift is a God-given ability through which the Holy Spirit supernaturally ministers to the body of Christ. Some scholars believe the Bible shows that we have just one gift, but that one gift can be a composite of various kinds of enablements that all come together to make the one unique gift that is ours alone. Others believe each of the enablements is a gift in itself.

Question 4. Growth in the use of our spiritual gifts often happens in two stages: the identification stage and the development stage. In the identification stage it is important to familiarize yourself with the different gifts and then try your hand at several different ministry areas to which you feel drawn. It is to your advantage to try new things because your experiences could uncover a gift you never knew you possessed!

The identification stage often takes several years and may involve a number of false starts before you will be able to say with certainty that you know what your gift is.

Question 8. Charles Ryrie, in writing about spiritual gifts, states, "If we are unwilling in any area, then God may not be able to use some gift; and conversely, if we are completely willing to do anything or go anywhere, the Lord may bring to light gifts which we never dreamed we had.... There are many who miss the full use of their gifts simply because they will not tie themselves down to a regular Sunday School class or even a simple administrative job in the church" (*Balancing the Christian Life,* Chicago, Ill.: Moody Press, 1969, p. 100).

Question 9. For further study:
> Flynn, Leslie B., *19 Gifts of the Spirit.* Wheaton, Ill.: Scripture Press, 1974.
> Frahm, David J., *The Great Niche Hunt.* Colorado Springs, Colo.: NavPress, 1991.

Study 4: Prepared for a Purpose

Question 8. "Countless explanations concerning the nature of Paul's thorn have been offered. They range from incessant temptation, dogged opponents, chronic maladies (such as opthalmia, malaria, migraine headaches, and epilepsy), to a disability of speech. No one can say for sure what it was, but it probably was a physical affliction" (Walvoord & Zuck, *The Bible Knowledge Commentary,* Wheaton, Ill.: Victor Books, 1983, p. 583).

Questions 10-11. The experience described in Hebrews 5:7 was "a form of education for Jesus before He served His suffering people.... He had to experience the true meaning of obedience in terms of the suffering it entailed. Having done so, He was thereby 'made perfect' for the role He would play as His people's Captain and High Priest.... It gave the already infinitely wise and perfect Son of God the experiential acquisition of knowledge about the human condition...and from it He can sympathize deeply with his followers" (*Bible Knowledge Commentary,* p. 792).

STUDY 5: IDENTIFYING GOD'S PURPOSES

Question 2. The passages from the book of Acts are accounts of Paul's conversion. This experience was inextricably intertwined with God's purpose for his life. (See also Acts 22:1-21.)

Question 4. The Phillips translation of Philippians 3:12 reads: "I do not consider myself to have 'arrived,' spiritually, nor do I consider myself already perfect. But I keep going on, grasping ever more firmly that purpose for which Christ Jesus grasped me."

Question 5. See Acts 26:12-18 for Paul's understanding of his specific life purpose.

Question 6. Here are some verses to consider as you begin to think through your overall life-purpose statement: Joshua 24:15, Micah 6:8, Matthew 6:33, Matthew 22:37-39, John 3:30, John 4:34, John 15:1-9, John 17:4, Acts 20:24, 1 Corinthians 10:31, and Philippians 3:10. For further reading on purposeful living, see *Living a Purpose-Full Life: What Happens When You Say Yes to God* by Jan Johnson (Colorado Springs, Colo.: WaterBrook Press, 1999).

Question 7. Here are some verses to consider as you identify the priority areas of your life:

- My Spiritual Life: Matthew 22:34-40; Psalms 19:7-14; 63:1-8.
- Home and Family: Titus 2:4-5; Colossians 3:12-21
- In the Church: 1 Corinthians 12:12-13, 27; Ephesians 4:11-16
- My Work: Genesis 1:26-31; 3:17-19; Ecclesiastes 5:18-20; Colossians 3:22-24

Note: If you have an extra week in your Bible study schedule, you may want to use it to give your group a chance to develop their purpose statements and then share them with one another. Encourage them to refer to the worksheet at the end of this book for writing out their ideas.

STUDY 6: PRIORITIES AND PLANNING

Question 2. It is easy to feel intimidated by the Proverbs 31 woman. Some explain her by saying that this is the description not of an actual woman but of a composite woman offered as an example of what we should be. Other commentators believe these verses don't list one woman's daily activities but identify what she accomplished throughout her lifetime.

Whatever the explanation, we need not feel either intimidated or limited by the accomplishments listed here. Some of us may feel we want to do more or less—or different things altogether. The main point is that this woman had a strong sense of what she was supposed to accomplish in her life, she understood that her contribution was valuable, and she disciplined herself to achieve her purposes.

Question 8. Example: If your life purpose is "to know God," your goals could be to spend fifteen minutes a day in Bible reading and prayer, to record your discoveries in a journal, and to join a small group Bible study at your church the next time one is offered. Notice that these goals are specific, accomplishable, and measurable.

Perhaps these steps will be helpful as you think through how to plan your goals:

a. Develop a written purpose statement that reflects your understanding of what God wants you to accomplish in an area, such as your spiritual life. (This is one aspect of your larger life-purpose statement addressed in Study 5.) You may want to break down this statement into different areas such as devotional life, character development, etc. List Scripture verses and passages that have contributed to your sense of purpose in these areas.

b. Reduce this purpose statement to specific goals (remember, a goal is measurable). For instance, if your purpose is to develop a more meaningful and consistent relationship with God, your goals may involve regular prayer and Bible reading times. If a specific aspect of your relationship needs attention (trust, worship, integrity, etc.), you may want to select a book, studyguide, or some other tool to assist you.

c. Think through the self-discipline you will need to accomplish these goals. What will you have to say yes to? What will you need to say no to? In the case of regular prayer time, you may decide that you need to cut out late-night television in order to get to bed earlier and get up earlier. You may have to set aside some less-important reading in order to focus on the study required.

d. Once you have developed your plan, keeping in mind the attitude expressed in James 4:15, pray that God will give you the strength and the discipline you need to accomplish his purposes.

Study 7: Exercising Discipline for a Purpose

Question 10. "Kingdom priorities might mean saying no to talking on the telephone so much. Or saying no to well-established committees in order to serve on other, more needy committees. Saying no to certain kinds of reading in order to do other, more crucial reading. Saying no to thinking so much about how you feel or the way you look—saying no to your pity parties.... It might mean limiting the time you spend thinking about fashion, shopping, romance, eating out, soap operas, novels, gossip, in order consciously to focus a certain amount of your thoughts on people's need for Jesus, on world hunger, on nuclear-weapon dangers, on teenage mothers" (Miriam Adeney, *A Time for Risking,* Portland, Oreg.: Mult-nomah Press, 1987, p. 56).

Study 8: God's Power for His Purposes

Question 5. In Exodus 3:14, God identifies himself to Moses as YHWH, which is the most significant name for God in the Old Testament. It means "the eternal, self-existent One" and "Israel's Redeemer." By using this name, God was reminding Moses that he was the only true God and that he was vitally interested in delivering his people.

Question 6. Moses' response in Exodus 4:13 may seem to us like an attractive expression of humility, but God did not regard it so. "When, in the face of the promises of God and the great truths he has revealed of himself, we persist in advancing our insufficiency as an excuse for avoiding our responsibilities, it is not a mark of humility but of unbelief" (Kenneth Pryor, *Perils of Leadership,* Downers Grove, Ill.: InterVarsity Press, 1990, p. 33).

A Life-Purpose Statement Worksheet

As you work through this studyguide, use the space below to record your thoughts regarding your life-purpose statement. The chart on the following page is an excellent place to jot down the goals and plans God lays on your heart as you think about how to live out his purposes in your life. (You may want to enlarge it on a photocopier to allow more space for writing.)

MY LIFE-PURPOSE STATEMENT:

LIFE CATEGORIES THROUGH WHICH I WILL LIVE OUT THIS PURPOSE STATEMENT:

	Mission	Goals	Disciplines
Relationship with God			
Family			
Work/Vocation			
Church/Community			
Physical Health and Well-being			
Recreation			
Personal Development (education, enrichment, travel, etc.)			
Other			

What Should We Study Next?

*T*o help your group answer that question, we've listed the Fisherman Studyguides by category so you can choose your next study.

TOPICAL STUDIES

Angels by Vinita Hampton Wright

Becoming Women of Purpose by Ruth Haley Barton

Building Your House on the Lord: Marriage and Parenthood by Steve and Dee Brestin

The Creative Heart of God: Living with Imagination by Ruth Goring

Discipleship: The Growing Christian's Lifestyle by James and Martha Reapsome

Doing Justice, Showing Mercy: Christian Actions in Today's World by Vinita Hampton Wright

Encouraging Others: Biblical Models for Caring by Lin Johnson

The End Times: Discovering What the Bible Says by E. Michael Rusten

Examining the Claims of Jesus by Dee Brestin

Friendship: Portraits in God's Family Album by Steve and Dee Brestin

The Fruit of the Spirit: Growing in Christian Character by Stuart Briscoe

Great Doctrines of the Bible by Stephen Board

Great Passages of the Bible by Carol Plueddemann

Great Prayers of the Bible by Carol Plueddemann

Growing Through Life's Challenges by James and Martha
    Reapsome

Guidance & God's Will by Tom and Joan Stark

Heart Renewal: Finding Spiritual Refreshment by Ruth
    Goring

Higher Ground: Steps Toward Christian Maturity by Steve
    and Dee Brestin

*Images of Redemption: God's Unfolding Plan Through the
    Bible* by Ruth Van Reken

Integrity: Character from the Inside Out by Ted Engstrom
    and Robert Larson

Lifestyle Priorities by John White

Marriage: Learning from Couples in Scripture by R. Paul
    and Gail Stevens

Miracles by Robbie Castleman

One Body, One Spirit: Building Relationships in the Church
    by Dale and Sandy Larsen

The Parables of Jesus by Gladys Hunt

Parenting with Purpose and Grace by Alice Fryling

Prayer: Discovering What the Bible Says by Timothy Jones
    and Jill Zook-Jones

The Prophets: God's Truth Tellers by Vinita Hampton
    Wright

Proverbs and Parables: God's Wisdom for Living by Dee
    Brestin

Satisfying Work: Christian Living from Nine to Five
    by R. Paul Stevens and Gerry Schoberg

Senior Saints: Growing Older in God's Family by James and
    Martha Reapsome

The Sermon on the Mount: The God Who Understands Me
     by Gladys Hunt
Spiritual Gifts by Karen Dockrey
Spiritual Hunger: Filling Your Deepest Longings by Jim and
     Carol Plueddemann
A Spiritual Legacy: Faith for the Next Generation by Chuck
     and Winnie Christensen
Spiritual Warfare by A. Scott Moreau
The Ten Commandments: God's Rules for Living by Stuart
     Briscoe
Ultimate Hope for Changing Times by Dale and Sandy
     Larsen
Who Is God? by David P. Seemuth
Who Is Jesus? In His Own Words by Ruth Van Reken
Who Is the Holy Spirit? by Barbara Knuckles and Ruth Van
     Reken
Wisdom for Today's Woman: Insights from Esther by Poppy
     Smith
Witnesses to All the World: God's Heart for the Nations
     by Jim and Carol Plueddemann
Women at Midlife: Embracing the Challenges by Jeanie
     Miley
Worship: Discovering What Scripture Says by Larry Sibley

BIBLE BOOK STUDIES

Genesis: Walking with God by Margaret Fromer and
     Sharrel Keyes
Exodus: God Our Deliverer by Dale and Sandy Larsen
Ezra and Nehemiah: A Time to Rebuild by James Reapsome

(For Esther, see Topical Studies, *Wisdom for Today's Woman*)

Job: Trusting Through Trials by Ron Klug

Psalms: A Guide to Prayer and Praise by Ron Klug

Proverbs: Wisdom That Works by Vinita Hampton Wright

Ecclesiastes: A Time for Everything by Stephen Board

Jeremiah: The Man and His Message by James Reapsome

Jonah, Habakkuk, and Malachi: Living Responsibly
by Margaret Fromer and Sharrel Keyes

Matthew: People of the Kingdom by Larry Sibley

Mark: God in Action by Chuck and Winnie Christensen

Luke: Following Jesus by Sharrel Keyes

John: The Living Word by Whitney Kuniholm

Acts 1–12: God Moves in the Early Church by Chuck and
Winnie Christensen

Acts 13–28, see *Paul* under Character Studies

Romans: The Christian Story by James Reapsome

1 Corinthians: Problems and Solutions in a Growing Church
by Charles and Ann Hummel

Strengthened to Serve: 2 Corinthians by Jim and Carol
Plueddemann

Galatians, Titus, and Philemon: Freedom in Christ
by Whitney Kuniholm

Ephesians: Living in God's Household by Robert Baylis

Philippians: God's Guide to Joy by Ron Klug

Colossians: Focus on Christ by Luci Shaw

Letters to the Thessalonians by Margaret Fromer and Sharrel
Keyes

Letters to Timothy: Discipleship in Action by Margaret
Fromer and Sharrel Keyes

Hebrews: Foundations for Faith by Gladys Hunt

James: Faith in Action by Chuck and Winnie Christensen

1 and 2 Peter, Jude: Called for a Purpose by Steve and Dee
 Brestin

How Should a Christian Live? 1, 2, and 3 John by Dee
 Brestin

Revelation: The Lamb Who Is a Lion by Gladys Hunt

BIBLE CHARACTER STUDIES

Abraham: Model of Faith by James Reapsome

David: Man After God's Own Heart by Robbie Castleman

Elijah: Obedience in a Threatening World by Robbie
 Castleman

Great People of the Bible by Carol Plueddemann

King David: Trusting God for a Lifetime by Robbie
 Castleman

Men Like Us: Ordinary Men, Extraordinary God by Paul
 Heidebrecht and Ted Scheuermann

Moses: Encountering God by Greg Asimakoupoulos

Paul: Thirteenth Apostle (Acts 13–28) by Chuck and
 Winnie Christensen

Women Like Us: Wisdom for Today's Issues by Ruth Haley
 Barton

Women Who Achieved for God by Winnie Christensen

Women Who Believed God by Winnie Christensen